PROTECT AND EMPOWER:

THE CAREER SURVIVAL GUIDE FOR HEALTHCARE PROFESSIONALS

INFO THAT MAY HELP YOU PROTECT YOUR LICENSE AND YOUR CAREER

Erica Lindsay PharmD, MBA, Esq.

ISBN: 978-1-941645-04-8

Designed and Published by:

Speakeasy Publications

73-03 Bell Blvd, #10
Oakland Gardens, NY 11364
www.SpeakeasyMarketingInc.com
888-225-8594

DISCLAIMER

This publication is intended to be informational only. No legal advice is being given, and no attorney-client relationship is intended to be created by reading this material. If you are facing legal issues, whether criminal or civil, seek professional legal counsel to get your questions answered.

Lindsay Law

420 N. May Street #205
Chicago, IL 60642
(312) 967-4484
www.4lindsaylaw.com

Table Of Contents

About The Author

Attorney Erica Lindsay has been practicing in healthcare for over 17 years. She has the unique skill set of having both the pharmacy expertise as well as the legal expertise. Erica provides counsel regarding healthcare operations, compliance and other healthcare legal matters.

Erica specializes in assisting healthcare practitioners involved with Employment Discrimination, License Defense and Fraud Disclosure/Retaliation Defense. She also represents both practitioners and patients in HIPAA violation cases.

HIPAA Law and Your Career

What Does HIPAA Stand For?

The Health Insurance Portability and Accountability Act, also known as "HIPAA", was approved through Congress in 1996. It provides the ability to have health coverage even through job transition. Previously, there may be a gap in coverage where a worker might have lost coverage in that transition period.

Additionally, HIPAA helps people gain access to their medical records. Previously, patients may be charged an exorbitant fee or have to wait a long time to get copies of their medical records. HIPAA allows for patients, with regulated law, to get their records easily at an affordable cost.

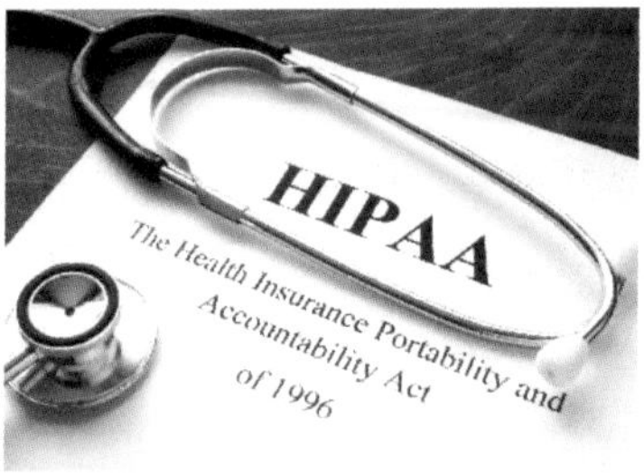

Finally, HIPAA assists with the electronic billing and establishes the industry standard for practitioners, facilities and providers to actually have a standard billing process for healthcare.

How Common Are HIPAA Violations?

HIPAA violations are quite common. There has been a major shift in how medical records are handled in more recent times. Years ago, healthcare employees could open the record of his or her mother, for example, or look at his or her child's record without any issue. Now, under HIPAA, healthcare employees are forbidden of such activities; it is against the law.

In fact, healthcare employees are not even allowed to access their own records. There has to be a reason to access someone's medical record which can be surrounded by many exceptions including by treatment, healthcare operations and payment. For example, if a practitioner handles a patient's treatment of care, healthcare operation surrounding that patient, or payment of that patient, the record can then be accessed.

- **Tip**: Employees should always disclose in writing to an employer or immediate supervisor prior to accessing their personal or a relative's medical record. If there is an audit to see why and when a patient's record was accessed, then the employee could be protected.

Another major violation is sharing medical information about a patient to a co-worker or another employee without an exception. For example, if a hospital administrator asks a nurse to look up a patient and tell them their status, this could be multiple violations. First, an employee should never look up a record on behalf of another. The person who accesses the record is ultimately responsible for the unauthorized access. Next, sharing medical information outside of an exception is illegal. I have seen many cases where a colleague or subordinate accessed a record for another without reason and it has led to direct termination.

- **Tip**: Another common violation is not logging off of the computer, allowing another person to view patient's Protected Health Information (PHI). The person logged in would be solely responsible.

People who must abide by HIPAA rules include healthcare providers, healthcare clearinghouses and healthcare plans. Healthcare practitioners and employee must be trained on how to properly access and handle records.

What Are The Common Misconceptions About HIPAA And HIPAA Violation Cases?

The most common misconceptions patients have regarding HIPAA and HIPAA violations are two-fold. Patients have claimed, "I'm going to sue you for HIPAA", and some attempt to file a civil claim. If the patient feels their records were viewed inappropriately by a healthcare employee or any third party that they have a cause of action to sue. Unfortunately, however, patients don't have a right to sue under HIPAA. Under HIPAA, the Department of Health and Human Services (HHS) manages the Office of Civil Rights (OCR) who can penalize the practitioners and/or the healthcare entity if a violation occurs however, usually no lawsuit can be filed by the patient directly.

However, if there is a claim of negligence on the part of the employee in handling the records and it involves a HIPAA violation, then that could possibly be actionable under the tort of negligence versus the actual HIPAA violation itself. HIPAA may be the underlying issue, however, it has to be a primary cause of neglect or any other tort that has occurred and then HIPAA can be mentioned within that cause of action.

WHAT ARE THE MOST COMMON TYPES OF HIPAA VIOLATION CASES?

The most common type of HIPAA violation is the mishandling of records. Mishandling records could include simple access of a patient's record electronically or an instance where information was shared with another person or company without permission. An example might be where a medical practitioner opens a medical record of a patient and then shares that information with another colleague without cause. In this case, there would be two breaches. The first breach is opening the medical record without exception and the second violation is sharing

that information with a colleague or a third party. Unfortunately, a lot of practitioners believe that they are helping the situation by consulting another colleague, when in fact that whole situation sets up a HIPAA breach.

Who Do You Represent In HIPAA Violation Cases?

For a healthcare practitioner, it is not necessarily a civil case brought on behalf of a patient trying to sue the practitioner. Most likely it would be dealing with the Board of Pharmacy, the Board of Nursing or the

Medical Board on behalf of the practitioner. If there is a HIPAA violation, then he or she could actually be reported to that respective board.

Many times, if a practitioner is found to be violating HIPAA laws, he or she may be terminated. If that happens, then the individual may need help through the unemployment process. It depends on the employer's rules and processes and how they handle HIPAA violations. Since many states are "at will" states, there is no protection for the employee who violates HIPAA and then is terminated.

- **Tip**: From the patient's perspective, if he or she has a case where the main tort is neglect, for example, HIPAA was somehow related to the actual case, then that would be something that could be explored further.

If there is a HIPAA breach, every healthcare entity has breach notification procedures to execute including reporting to the patient, the media, as well as reporting to the OCR, the division under HHS that handles all HIPAA violations. For example, if there was a breach where a laptop was stolen with PHI, that information now is vulnerable and that entity has to contact everyone whose information is compromised. Patient remedies may include identity fraud protection for one year or more to protect them. However, the fine to the entity would be assessed by the OCR and the entity would not give actual payment to the violated patients.

HOW CAN SOMEONE REPORT A HIPAA VIOLATION?

The agency that handles HIPAA violations is the Office for Civil Rights (OCR) housed under Health & Human Services within the government. If a patient wishes to file a complaint, they can do so by going to U.S. Department of Health & Human Services website where they will find all of the instructions listed on how to file a HIPAA breach.

If an employee needs to report a colleague, there are several ways to file. One way is by filing a complaint with a direct supervisor about the incident. The supervisor can request a computer audit trail to validate unauthorized access. Another way of reporting an incident can be by going through the healthcare facility's compliance department, and you should have the option to file anonymously, if desired.

Lastly, a report can be filed with the government as well, however this may take a little bit longer because they will have to locate the records and contact employees within the facility.

What Further Steps Does Someone Need To Take If They Are A Victim Of A HIPAA Violation?

In most cases, patients do not know they are a victim of a HIPAA violation because typically it is not something that occurs directly in front of him or her.

However, if for instance a patient, Jane Green gets the wrong medication and it is labeled "Jane Green" however, with a different birthday that could be something where one could say, "Well, my information was disclosed to the wrong Jane Green and I want to file a report".

In a situation such as this if someone wants to capture that violation, the individual should take notes and write down exactly what happened and who was involved. Then file a report with either the entity or OCR.

Now if it was an incident such as the laptop being stolen out of a facility and patient's PHI was stored on there, he or she wouldn't be aware of the violation until the entity contacted him or her. Once that contact occurs, the entity would inform the patient. It can be a challenge to identify what the patient can do in these cases because again, he or she does not usually know a violation has occurred until afterwards. Criminals can use stolen PHI information to file fraudulent tax returns or Medicaid claims for profit. In these situations, violated patients wouldn't become aware that a HIPAA violation had occurred until after the fact and may only find out if the IRS or HHS contact the patient directly. HIPAA also applies to employee information; the healthcare entity is responsible for the protection of that information as well.

How Is A HIPAA Violation Situation Remedied?

Remedies to HIPAA violations depend on what the violation is. If someone unauthorized is accessing a record and there is fear of future identity theft, the entity may decide to help pay for identity theft coverage for the person or group of people whose information was breached.

Healthcare entities may have insurance to cover HIPAA violations; however, this does not necessarily give money directly to the patient. The insurance will cover the fees or fines assessed by the Office for Civil Rights, the mailing to the patient, the identity theft coverage and may improve the infrastructure to prevent another HIPAA breach.

How Is The Viability Of A HIPAA Violation Case Determined?

There are only a handful of HIPAA violation cases that have been successful under the tort of negligence. In one Indiana case, a pharmacist accessed the prescription records of her husband's alleged mistress and told her husband that she had an STD. In that case, the victim filed under negligence even though the disclosure of information was a HIPAA violation. The victim was awarded $1.44 million, however; it was a very unique case. The pharmacist intentionally accessed the patient's record and then shared the health information to someone outside of the entity and the access was for an unauthorized use. This was such an egregious case that the jury found in favor for the plaintiff.

How Important Are Evidence And Witnesses In HIPAA Violation Cases?

Evidence is important. When someone accesses an electronic medical record (EMR), the access is recorded and can be audited anytime. The record creates evidence of when the HIPAA breach occurred. Even if the person logged on is not the actual person who accessed the record, they will be held ultimately responsible. The actual breach is memorialized in an audit, is a key piece of evidence that can be used in terminating an employee.

Experienced attorneys knowledgeable in HIPAA can discern if the case facts would lend to a successful negligence case based on HIPAA violation(s). However, attorneys who lack experience with HIPAA law may be unsuccessful in prosecuting the case.

Who Can Be Held Responsible For A HIPAA Violation?

The healthcare entity is ultimately responsible for HIPAA violations because they are responsible for the actions of their employees when they are working for them under the legal doctrine, Respondent Superior. In the example of the pharmacist who accessed the record of her husband's girlfriend, the pharmacist was technically found responsible. However, the victim filed against Retailer and the pharmacist because Retailer was the employer and was found directly liable for pharmacist's actions.

What Damages Can Be Awarded In A HIPAA Violation Case?

Once a negligence case with HIPAA violation(s) is identified, there has to be actual damages to be actionable in court. For example, if a prescription for an allergy for a "Jane Green" was given to the wrong Jane Green, that's not going to show damages because the medication that is being prescribed is not any type of "embarrassment" to the patient. However, if the patient takes a prescription for HIV medication and that is given to the wrong Jane Green and she tells people that know the patient knows that she has HIV, that example would be an argument for damages. When it is something insignificant, such as allergy medication versus a HIV medication, it is easy to understand there is a different level of sensitivity.

How Long Do HIPAA Violation Cases Take To Resolve?

If a case is presented in front of the judge and he or she understands HIPAA regulations, then the case can be decided relatively quickly through summary judgment.

If it's a case that actually has actionable cause that could be pursued, then it could be a civil case which depends on the jurisdiction.

However, little or no damages are identified and there is no harm to the patient, the case may be dismissed quickly.

Healthcare License Defense

Who Can File A Licensing Board Complaint?

Anyone can file a licensing board complaint, including patients, family representatives or employers. If you work for a healthcare entity, the complaint could be directed against you,

your colleagues or the institution. For example, if a nurse sees something that is unethical, she can file a complaint against a colleague, whether it's another pharmacist, a technician, a physician or a nurse. Anyone can file a complaint.

What Are The Most Common Reasons For Licensing Board Complaints To Be Filed?

There are extremes when it comes to complaints. The most extreme claim would be wrongful death. If a family representative feels that a practitioner caused the wrongful death of their loved one, they would be able to file a complaint. Filing a complaint involves administrative law, the government branch who manages professional licenses. If the healthcare practitioner is accused of criminal acts, the case will be held in criminal court.

An example of a complaint generated by the board would be the practitioner not fulfilling all of their

Continuing Education (CE) requirements. The most predominant issues seen with medical professionals involve the following: non-payment of taxes; non-payment of child support; and falsification of records. However, you need someone to be an advocate for you when it comes to board complaints.

What Are The Top Misconceptions About The Licensing Board Complaint Process?

If a complaint is received, the licensee may ignore it or delay their response. Anytime a licensee receives notification from their healthcare licensing board, they should respond immediately.

The administrative law department will normally send a letter to the practitioner regarding any issues that have been reported to the board e.g., complaints. To avoid penalties when it comes to not responding in a timely manner, licensees should make sure that their address is current with their professional board. If the licensee's address isn't current, and the notice is sent without a response, the department will proceed against the practitioner without representation. If the practitioner does not respond in a timely manner, the proceeding will continue and can lead to an adverse action against them. Once the proceeding has been completed, the results can be posted online.

There is a chance the practitioner will not know a judgment is filed against them until they try to renew their license. The online reporting system informs the public of disciplinary actions taken against a healthcare provider along with any issues that the board found in the investigation. If the provider finds out that there is an adverse action against their license and they are unable to renew, contact an attorney immediately for assistance.

Are There Many Attorneys That Practice Healthcare License Defense?

There are many attorneys that practice healthcare license defense, which falls under administrative law. According to AVVO, there are currently 1,900 attorneys licensed in Illinois. However, there are very few that have a medical background. If you are a healthcare practitioner, it's to your advantage to find someone who has a medical background because an attorney with a medical background can provide better protections from exposure. If you hire a typical administrative law attorney, they may be handling various other types of cases and won't be able to offer you the healthcare expertise in your defense.

ARE CERTAIN MEDICAL PROFESSIONALS MORE AT RISK THAN OTHERS?

Physicians are always a target because they are the ones who are primarily responsible for the patient's care. Usually, with physicians who are employed by the hospital, they may carry their own medical malpractice insurance and have their own legal counsel. Other healthcare professionals, pharmacists, nurses, etc. may have insurance provided by their employer.

By the insurance being provided by the employer, the employer will have the best representation, not the employee covered by the insurance provided by the entity.

- **Tip**: The attorney's duty of care and duty of loyalty is towards the employer, the entity who actually hired them. If there is a conflict between the employer and the practitioner, that attorney may not be the best fit for the practitioner. A practitioner may need to retain an attorney that serves their interests.

How Are People Generally Notified Once A Complaint Is Filed?

The medical board or state agency can contact the practitioner through the mail, email or phone. Mail is the traditional form of contract, however, sometimes the practitioner may receive the notice and sometimes they may not.

- **Tip**: It is crucial to keep your contact information up-to-date with the agency. They can also contact you via email or phone, so it's best to make sure all contact information is up-to-date as well.

How Public Will Be The Knowledge Of A Licensing Board Complaint?

The Board hearings that deal with discipline licensure issues are usually held in a closed meeting. Usually when a practitioner appears before the board members, those hearings are private. Many decisions that are made in the private hearing become public through the online reporting system.

How Should A Licensee Respond When They Learn About A Licensing Board Complaint?

The response generally depends on the action. The agency may contact a practitioner to gather information or a clarification of an issue. However, if the agency is requesting any information that might put you at risk for discipline, it would be wise to get an attorney to assess the situation to determine if you need representation to protect your interest. This will keep you from inadvertently disclosing information to the agency that could be later on held against you in any type of proceeding.

- **Tip**: If you discuss any issues with an attorney, you will be protected by attorney-client privilege. If it is basic information, give it to the investigator. If it is information that might put you at risk or you're not sure if it will, talk to an attorney.

How Long Does Someone Have To Address A Complaint?

The time period is determined by the board's policies and procedures. The board will notify the licensee requesting information. The board will review the requested information stated in the correspondence sent to the licensee. You don't want to miss the deadline; once you get that notice in hand, make sure that you are compliant with the deadlines given.

What Happens If Someone Ignores Or Misses The Deadline?

The board or agency will continue with their investigation. The key is that if the licensee is not represented, they will proceed with the case based on the information they have. It's unfortunate when the licensee

is not able to represent themselves before the board during the decision process. However, the board usually makes decisions based on precedent and the rules and regulations established by each board.

Is A Licensee Required To Notify Anyone In This Process?

You should disclose to your employer any type of final adverse action against your license. If you don't and the employer finds out, even if you keep your license, you may be terminated. The entity must comply with the rules and regulations of all federal/state agencies, which require that every practitioner must have an active license. If your license is revoked, you may be terminated.

Should A Licensee Ever Discuss Their Complaint With The Complainant In This Process?

Under no circumstances should a licensee discuss their complaint with the complainant. For example a family member files a complaint regarding wrongful death; you don't want to reach out directly to the person who filed the complaint. That exposes you. In those types of situations, definitely have your attorney handle all communications. However, if it's something that's not that extreme, you still want to protect yourself and not reach out to the person who filed the complaint. You may reach out to the board for guidance; however that can also put you at risk.

Can A Licensee Ever Discuss Their Complaint With Family Or Friends?

It depends. If you have a spouse and you discuss the issue with them your communications may be legally protected. However, it's not wise to share information regarding licensing issues with family or friends because you don't know how that information could be disclosed to others and be used adversely against you. It's the same for colleagues; it just makes the licensee more vulnerable to potential issues down the road.

Can A Licensee Call The Board's Regulatory Or Investigative Authority To Discuss The Complaint?

If you don't hire an attorney, you can call the board's regulatory or investigative authority. However, keep in mind that you're putting yourself at risk as whatever you disclose could be passed on to the board members, attorneys, law enforcement, etc. because there is no confidentiality between you the licensee and the board representative. If the information requested can put your license at risk, it's not advisable to talk to the representative directly. It's best to talk to your attorney, because they can provide a layer of protection between you and the board. The attorney can get the information needed without exposing the licensee which is the ultimate goal.

How Should A Licensee Respond On Being Contacted By The Board?

The response depends on what the contact is regarding from the Board. Usually, the board will contact you by phone or through the mail. If it's through the mail and you can resolve it yourself, provide the requested information. If the board calls you and says, "We would like to see you," or they come to your home or place of employment, that is probably where you would want the legal protections provided by an attorney.

- **Tip**: If you are not able to prepare a quality response for the investigator, I would say, "Speak to my attorney," because you need those protections.

Is The Job Of The Licensing Board To Look Out For The Interests Of Licensed Professionals?

No. The job of the licensing board is to protect the interests of the public. If the licensee is found to be in violation or a danger to the public in any way, the medical board or agency would most likely precede suspending or terminating the practitioner's license. Possessing a license issued by a healthcare board is a privilege and the board agency could suspend it at any time. Each board varies by state in terms of licensing, and licenses can be terminated at any time based on the public interest.

What Can A Licensee Expect During The Investigative Process Conducted By The Board?

The investigative process depends on how extensive the complaint is. If it is a wrongful death complaint, you will have a lot of interaction with the investigators, attorneys and the board; you might have several meetings on the phone and in person. If it is a common violation that is easily resolved, the board will follow established policy and the procedures to resolve the issue. However, the more unique the offense is, the more guidance there will be from the Board's or agency's attorney.

Can A Licensee Keep Working During The Investigative Process?

If you're under investigation and the board or the agency has not made a determination against your license, you can still continue to work. Once the state or federal agency has made a determination against your license you should disclose to your employer, again because you have other issues that put them at risk. So as long as there has not been any action taken against your license, you should be able to work.

What Are The Common Mistakes Committed By Licensees In This Process?

Some practitioners can become overwhelmed by the process. Others may ignore the notice because they don't want to jeopardize their job, or they will call the board and just start telling them everything that happened. Any communication between the practitioner and the board is not protected. Those are the common mistakes made.

This is especially true with the licensee who ignores the complaint; they may say, "I'm just going to hopefully let this blow over" because they're intimidated by talking to an attorney or to the agency.

As a healthcare practitioner, you need to understand your rights. When you talk to an investigator or with the board, keep in mind those calls could be recorded, so you don't want to expose yourself. Anything that has been stated to a representative of an agency could be detrimental to you later on in a hearing.

What Type Of Disciplinary Action Can The Licensing Board Take?

There are various disciplinary actions a licensing board can take. One example from Illinois is: Refuse to Renew. This judgment allows a practitioner to keep their license active up until its expiration. For instance, if a practitioner had their license active until June 30th, 2016, under Refuse to Renew, come July 1st, they could not renew their license and would have to clear an outstanding matter with the board before they were granted the right to renew their license.

Another disciplinary action is suspension. The board could suspend your license for any period of time. For instance, if a practitioner is suspended for 30 days, under the suspension, she can't practice. After the 30 days, it is safe to practice.

If one does practice during the suspension, any Federal insurance claims within that window of 30 days would be seen as false claims, and that brings in other issues, so you don't want to put yourself or your employer at risk.

Finally, there is termination. A license is a privilege, not a right. When your license is terminated, that means that you cannot practice.

Many times, there are license terminations or suspensions from sister states. Each state has its own licensing board. However, for instance, you are licensed in three states. If one of these licenses is suspended, the other two states could suspend or terminate your license because of the action taken in the first state. The board has the discretion to levy any other type of disciplinary action it may so choose.

Does Your Firm Provide Legal Assistance With License Renewal Processes?

Yes. Retaining an attorney early in the process makes the process much easier. However, if you hire them after the fact, whether it's after a suspension or after the license is denied, it's an uphill battle. The attorney would attempt to undo the process versus being proactive. However, it's much more difficult after the determination's already been done to undo it.

Why Should Someone Hire An Attorney To Deal With A Licensing Complaint?

As a practitioner, you may not understand the legal protections that are afforded to you. The board is for the public interest. By hiring an attorney, you have attorney-client privilege where you can explain the situation freely, which then allows the attorney to craft and protect you, as well as communicate with the board, the agency or law enforcement to resolve the matter. You can resolve many matters legally without exposure, which ideally prevents your livelihood from being taken away. In those situations, it's very easy to say, "Let me just try to call and fix it," however sometimes this makes matters worse.

What Should Someone Be Prepared For After Contacting An Attorney?

The attorney is there to support the provider through listening and understanding to their client's needs. Retaining an attorney would depend on the magnitude of the case. If the licensee needs to retain counsel for representation, payment can be paid through a retainer. The charges can be through a flat fee or hourly rate.

- **Tip**: Before the meeting with the attorney write down the facts for your own recollection; so when you're speaking to the attorney, you're able to disclose as many facts as you can because if you go off memory, you will forget things. Those things that you forget could actually hurt you down the road. Being concise and complete is a key to all communications to your attorney.

If you prepare for your meeting with the attorney, you'll be able to communicate in a calm manner. Once you have communicated the facts to the attorney, the attorney should take it from there as far as telling you the next steps, in terms of what they're going to do, the structure of the process and the expectations. If you have a good attorney, you should then have the peace of mind to know that "Yes, this is now being handled. Now, I can continue to practice," because again, if you're practicing under stress, it could lead to further issues and problems down the road.

What Should I Be Looking For In An Attorney When I Have A Licensing Board Complaint To Deal With?

If you're a healthcare practitioner, I would say look for someone who actually practices healthcare law. If they don't practice healthcare law, you're going to be at a disadvantage because they are not going to know operations within a healthcare system, whether it's a pharmacy, nursing home or a hospital. So if you're a healthcare practitioner, you want someone who can speak the same lingo and give you those protective interests to prevent you from exposure. Even if you get an eminent law attorney, they may not be able to give you that insight and could cause you to be exposed more than needed.

Termination Or License Discipline Resulting From Use Of Medical Marijuana

Can healthcare practitioners, who have a qualifying medical condition, be allowed to use medical marijuana to help treat that condition without being in jeopardy of losing their job or their license? It is a sticky situation because under federal law, marijuana is a controlled substance, which means it's illegal, and you don't have those protections available under state law declaring patients can use medical marijuana if you have cancer, multiple sclerosis, or any other qualifying condition. Medical marijuana has been licensed for qualifying medical conditions currently in 26 states.

Healthcare practitioners handle patients all the time, however, when a practitioner is afflicted, how are they able to take advantage of those opportunities that the states have granted? Right now, it is a conflict. Currently, if a practitioner is using medical marijuana and the employer does a drug test that comes up positive, the practitioner can be terminated, especially if it is at-will employment.

States including California and Washington State have taken the stance that the employer can terminate an employee for medical marijuana usage. As far as licensing is concerned, each license branch is its own entity and can suspend or terminate their license anytime. Anytime a practitioner is looking to get legal defense for their license, it's important for the administrative law attorney to actually have insight to know again how to protect them from exposure.

Employment Law and Wrongful Termination

What Is Employment Law?

Employment law is regulated by federal and state agencies. Each state does have its own specific employment laws; however, they all have to abide at minimum with the federal law.

How Is "Employment At Will" Defined?

Employees who do not have a written contract protecting their employment interest are "at-will" employees. This means an employer can fire him or her for any reason. For employees who do have a written contract, the contract would protect him or her from being terminated for no cause which could be enforced by the court. If there is no contract, however, then the employee can be terminated for any reason unless prohibited under state law.

Can An "At Will" Employee Be Fired For Any Reason?

Every organization should have policies and procedures they follow regarding employees and termination. Human Resources (HR) should follow their established

policies and procedures in the termination of an employee. HR has policies that streamline the termination process and normally if it is a warning process the individual could get a first warning, second warning and then ultimately be terminated. HR must follow the policies and terminate employees consistently; there cannot be a variation in the termination of employees.

Are Most People Aware Of These Laws?

No, many employees do not realize how vulnerable they are until they are in an HR situation. Today's work environment has changed. Previously, there were certain levels of respect between employees and employers. Currently, it is a more aggressive work environment. It is more challenging and there are no guarantees. This is especially true for older employees who may have started off with a company and worked there over 20 years and then all of a sudden, they get disciplined for no reason leading to termination.

Whether management doesn't have the same morals and ethics that previous managers possess or newer managers have a different perspective and expectation, employment cannot be taken lightly. It's unfortunate because someone who dedicates their career by working over 20 years for a company would get a person's loyalty back. Now, there is no guarantee for that. People don't think about it. They are usually content to have a job and they don't know how to protect themselves while employed.

What Does Wrongful Termination Mean?

Wrongful termination, also known as wrongful dismissal, occurs when an employee has been terminated unfairly either through contract terms or by statute provision of employment law. Wrongful dismissal varies according to the terms of the employers' contracts and by each state's jurisdiction. Wrongful termination simply means that the employer erroneously terminated the employee.

There are remedies to wrongful termination. The individual who is wrongfully dismissed can file a case against his or her employer and if the court favors the claimant, he or she may be entitled to back pay and reinstatement.

What Are The Common Statutes Protecting People From Termination?

There are no true protections from wrongful termination other than the protections afforded by the Federal laws. The U.S. Equal Employment Opportunity Commission (EEOC) is responsible for enforcing federal laws that make it illegal to discriminate against a job applicant or an employee because of the person's race, color, religion, sex (including pregnancy, gender identity, and sexual orientation), national origin, age (40 or older), disability, equal pay or genetic information. It is also illegal to discriminate against a person because the person complained about discrimination, also known as retaliation. Below is a list of the major employment laws which create protected status for certain employees:

- Americans with Disabilities Act (ADA) and the ADA Amendments Act (prohibits discrimination because of a job applicant or employee's disability)
- Age Discrimination in Employment Act (ADEA) (prohibits discrimination based on age)
- Title VII of the Civil Rights Act of 1964 (prohibits discrimination based on several different characteristics)
- Civil Rights Act of 1866, Section 1981 (prohibits discrimination because of race in contracts)
- COBRA (federal law regarding health insurance coverage continuation)
- Employee Retirement Income Security Act (ERISA) (prohibits discrimination in employee retirement plans)
- Fair Labor Standards Act (FLSA) (federal law regarding wage and hour issues)
- Family and Medical Leave Act (FMLA) (federal law providing job-protected family and medical leave)

- National Labor Relations Act (NLRA) (federal law governing labor relations)
- Occupational Safety and Health Act (OSHA) (federal law regarding workplace health and safety)
- Older Workers Benefit Protection Act (OWPBA) (protects older workers benefits from age discrimination)
- Pregnancy Discrimination Act (PDA) (prohibits discrimination based on pregnancy, childbirth or related conditions)
- Rehabilitation Act
- Sarbanes-Oxley Act (protects workers who are whistleblowers)
- Uniformed Services Employment and Reemployment Rights Act (USERRA) (prohibits discrimination against members of the armed forces)
- Worker Adjustment and Retraining Notification Act (WARN Act) (layoff notification law)

What Is The Best Way To Prove A Discrimination Claim?

The best way to address a discrimination claim is through a class action suit. A trend of terminations targeting a particular group of people can establish a class action case. For instance, if a person feels they were terminated because they are old, that is going to be very hard to prove. However, if older employees are being terminated without cause, that can illustrate a trend to the court that could prove strong evidence of discrimination.

The key in these cases is to gather several examples against the particular employer with the same instance that will show the trend.

- **Tip**: Document what happens at work, even if it seems benign at the time. Keeping a handwritten daily journal showing what is happening while at work can be invaluable. If you choose to use a computer to document daily activities, use your personal computer with a date and time stamp. Do not use your work computer because that information can be accessed by the employer and after termination, you will not have access to those files. Having a daily journal can provide credibility to the claimant.

Once an HR issue is brought to the employee, the employee can provide historical notes to HR to provide a level of protection illustrating what has happened during their time of employment.

A single employee can file a successful discrimination claim, however the discriminatory acts have to be clear and distinct and documented. If not, it may be an uphill battle, especially working in an "at will" state.

What Factors Determine A Viable Claim Against An Employer?

The factors that make up a viable claim against an employer vary based on the reason someone was terminated for. Arrange a consultation with an attorney to discuss the circumstances surrounding the termination; whether they are currently employed or they have been terminated. They listen to the facts to understand how to proceed as every case is handled differently.

Are Cases Where Someone Is Fired Because Of A Criminal Record Handled Differently?

Many have reported to be discriminated against because of a criminal record. There are no federal protections that can prevent an employer from not hiring someone if they have a criminal record.

In the healthcare industry especially, if someone has a criminal record or if has been convicted of fraud, that information has to be disclosed. That individual most likely won't be hired because the organization must stay compliant with the

federal and state guidelines. The organization cannot hire people convicted of Medicaid fraud to handle Medicare or Medicaid claims, for example.

That being said, a criminal conviction is something that could hurt any type of employment.

There are some state laws that prohibit discrimination of criminal records.

What Kind Of Damages Can Someone Recover From A Successful Lawsuit Against An Employer?

In situations where the employee refused to commit an illegal act or the employer doesn't follow consistent termination are examples that can lead to damages. Damages can be nominal or punitive. For example, it is common for an employee to be placed on paid administrative leave while the incident or claims are investigated.

However, if the reason for termination was based on discrimination, retaliation, or refusing to commit an illegal act, damages can be sought and awarded. If the termination was egregious, punitive damages against the employer may be available as well. All filings are determined on a case by case basis.

How Do I Know If I Need An Attorney For A Wrongful Termination Suit?

When filing a claim, especially against a large employer, any individual may need legal guidance.

Can Someone File For Unemployment Compensation During A Pending Termination Case?

In order to receive unemployment compensation, the individual has to have been terminated or laid off. Usually when someone is at an unemployment hearing, the adjudicator or the judge will determine if the employee was terminated or did the employee resign from the position.

When the employer states that the employee was terminated, that can start the unemployment claim. A claimant can pursue an unemployment claim while filing a federal or state discrimination suit.

Does Someone Still Have A Case If They Accepted A Severance Package At Termination?

If someone accepts a severance package, they may still be able to pursue a wrongful termination case. When someone accepts a severance package, the contract could have certain restrictions stating that the individual is waiving the right to file a claim against the employer. If the termination was for discrimination or retaliation, the organization cannot force anyone to waive the right to file a claim; it's a federally protected issue.

How Do I Know Who Is The Right Kind Of An Attorney For A Wrongful Termination Case?

The selected attorney should have the ability to view an issue from both the perspective of the healthcare practitioner and the legal context.

Having a good attorney/client relationship is essential. The success of a case is based on how well the individual and his or her attorney connect.

Here are several helpful hints to share for clients when dealing with situations in the workplace.

1. Keep a copy of the company's human resource manual at home. If something happens to where an individual is terminated quickly and removed off the premises, at least he or she will have the HR manual at home for reference.

2. Keeping a log of daily activities. If nothing happens, just record "No incident" in a handwritten journal. If an incident does occur, record the date, what happened, who was involved or who witnessed the incident, etc.

3. If an individual decides to leave his or her employment, he or she should always ask their supervisor if they intend to mark his or her file as a re-hire. If a person resigns and their supervisor does not mark him or her as a re-hire, that's basically a blackball.

   Additionally, if the employee has signed a non-compete clause when hired, it should be understood what exactly that means. If a person is terminated, how does that not-compete clause actually affect their future employment? For example, can someone still go work with a competing facility if he or she was terminated or does the individual's new employment have to be outside of a certain distance of the former employer?

- **Tip**: It is always advisable to review your contract prior to signing with an attorney who specializes in healthcare contract law.

4. For a licensed practitioner, he or she should always keep his or her file current and always check with the board to be sure if there are any complaints against his or her license. There are times when complaints can be filed unknown to the practitioner. If there are any complaints, one should be sure to address those as quickly as possible.

5. Take a test run before committing to a new position. That first look of employment shows the true colors of a supervisor, colleagues and work environment. Before resigning from a position, understand what could be the atmosphere at the new job. Take some time off or a leave of absence if possible, to see how the new position and company will work out. If the individual doesn't like it, then he or she won't have any problems going back to his or her job.

6. Change his or her status to PRN. This is one of the great things about being a healthcare practitioner. An individual doesn't necessarily have to quit, however, instead change his or her status to PRN as needed. Physicians, nurses, pharmacists and other healthcare practitioners can explore that option.

SPECIAL THANKS

I dedicate my first published book to my husband, Eddie Lindsay. He has been amazing during this journey and we have many more adventures to look forward to.